A Window into Heaven

Gale Nemec

Photographed by
Joy Nemec Loper

ISBN: 978-1-947608-23-8

Copyright © 2021 -2025
All Rights Reserved
Nemec LLC
Alexandria, Virginia, USA
www.GaleNemecBooks.com

Edited by
Martha Newman

Dedicated to
Our creator, sunrises, and sunsets,
senior citizens, teens, my
wonderful readers and to taking
a moment to look up and
become absorbed in the sky.

This book belongs to

_____

This book is from

_____

Today's Date

_____

I had a bad day,
was beyond sad.
I could think of nothing
that would make
me glad.

The sun was setting
So, I looked out to see
a dazzling sunset.
It was meant for me.

Filled with streaks of
orange,
pink and gold
and countless other colors
too numerous to be told.

The vast sky showed me
a window into heaven.
God's beautiful gift,
days one through seven.

The sky was stunning
as each color appeared.
I couldn't believe my eyes
it was all so clear.

Its splendor gave me joy
and happiness, too.
Suddenly I realized
I could not be blue.

As I watched
this incredible,
fast-moving sky
with colors so brilliant,
I could not deny...

...each color was striking,
and radiant, too!
Lost in my thoughts
all I could do...

...was stand in awe
and truly see
this peek into heaven
meant for me.

It filled me with wonder
and made me slow down.
I suddenly realized
what could be found.

How heaven could look
how it could be,
when I passed from
this life
to be with Thee.

A window into heaven,
days one through seven.
Sunsets and sunrises
stunning to see.
Oh! What peace, joy,
serenity, and faith it gives
to me.

ABOUT THE AUTHOR

Gale Nemec is an award-winning producer, actress, and voice talent. She created and produced *The Bea & the Bug* an award winning, multimedia, interactive musical show. She is currently working on a new series, *Adventures in Time, a time-travel series for kids* featuring American history.

ABOUT THE PHOTOGRAPHER

Joy Nemec Loper has an excellent eye for sunsets, sunrises, and nature's beauty. When looking at her vibrant, natural photographs, one can almost hear the ocean gently rolling on the shore, a few birds at sunset and the perfect silence of the moon floating in the night sky. Joy always has a camera near-by, so she is able to preserve moments of God's splendor.

BACK COVER PHOTO

Gale Nemec by: Betsy Royall
Betsy Royall Photography
Joy Nemec Loper by: Charles Loper

HOLIDAY BOOKS
Little Stockey & the Miracle of Christmas
Valentine Cards for the Christian Faith
Valentine Cards for Valentine's Day

BILINGUAL: SPANISH AND ENGLISH
Hay un Oso en La Banca
(There's a Bear on a Bench)

SPANISH
El pequeño Stockey y el Milagro
de la Navidad
(Little Stockey & the Miracle
of Christmas)

INTERACTIVE BOOKS ON YOUTUBE
There's a Bear on a Bench
Throwing Rocks in the River

NON-FICTION
Caught in the Crosshairs of War

VIDEOS FOR THE WHOLE FAMILY

Live! Little Stockey & the
Miracle of Christmas

Animals & Music Volume 1
Animals & Music Volume 2
Animals & Music Volume 3
Animals & Music Volume 4
Animals & Music Volume 5

This book is a perfect gift for any age
and any occasion.

Enjoy writing a review
on Amazon and social media, too.

What shapes do you see in the clouds?

www.ingramcontent.com/pod-product-compliance
Lightning Source LLC
Chambersburg PA
CBHW042120060426
42446CB00038B/53